I0168049

ODDS AND ENDS

ODDS AND ENDS

Farrell R. Davisson

REBEL SATORI PRESS

NEW ORLEANS

Published in the United States of America by
REBEL SATORI PRESS
www.rebelsatori.com

Copyright © 2021 by the estate of Farrell R. Davisson. All rights reserved.
Except for brief passages quoted in newspaper, magazine, radio, television,
or online reviews, no part of this book may be reproduced in any form or
any means, electronic or mechanical, including photocopying, recording,
or information or retrieval system, without the permission in writing
from the publisher. Please do not participate in or encourage piracy of
copyrighted materials in violation of the author's rights. Purchase only
authorized editions.

Select poems have appeared previously in *Kennebec: A Portfolio of Maine
Writing, Maine Times.*

Edited by Sven Davisson.

Library of Congress Control Number: 2021932747

Contents

Davisson interviews Kukla and Ollie of the eponymous 50s TV show
(not sure where Fran was that day)

Farrell Robert Davisson

Born March 27, 1919 in Rock Valley, a small farming community in the northwest corner of Iowa, Farrell R. Davisson was descended from a mid western mix of Scottish, Norwegian, English, and Irish immigrants. During World War II, Davisson joined the US Merchant Marine. On the eve of shipping out, he was diagnosed with tuberculosis and spent the remainder of the war as a patient at Oakdale Sanatorium in Iowa City. While a patient, he was able to attend the University of Iowa's writing program as a correspondent. Following the introduction of civilian use of penicillin in 1945, Davisson moved to Chicago and began his career as a reporter. He would describe himself during this time as "one of the scarce *goyim* on the Chicago staff of *Variety* who covered the birth and death of television back in the Trojan Fifties" He eventually rose to city desk editor at the Chicago bureau of *Daily Variety*. After a time, he relocated to the Maine coast where he continued to work as a freelance journalist while focusing on his creative writing. Additioanlly, after a stint teaching journalism at Penn State, he continued to mentor young journalists throughout the rest of his life. In 1993 Davisson succumbed to cancer—a condition that had long fascinated him and had been a recurrent subject in his writing.

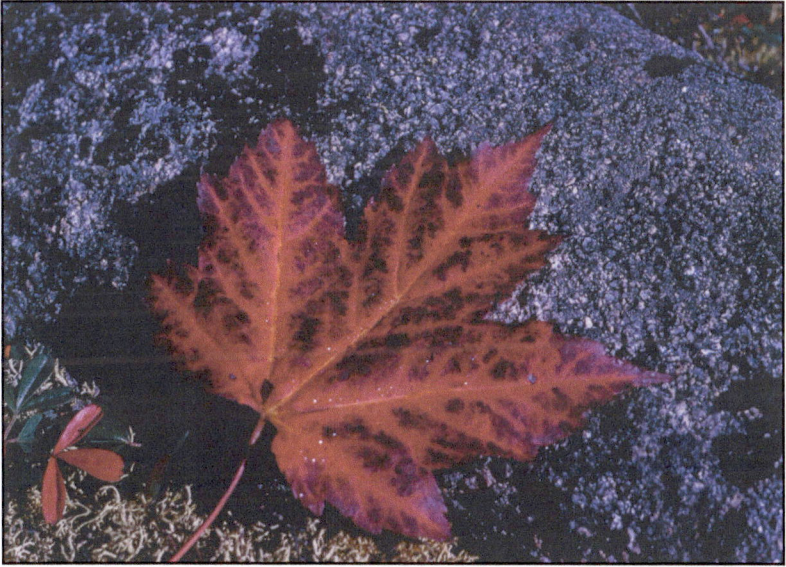

Odds and Ends

Already burnished
a ceremonial bronze,
the tardy oak leaf,
cued by the gale's
ending rattle, abandons
its roots to spiral
one last whimsical
heavenward tack until,
succumbing to gravity,
returns its mite
to the teeming
debris below.

Pull & Haul

Poets, true
lovers, heed the sea:
that constant beckoning to
flee staid landings
      until old bearings
      are lost,
looming anew in the deeps
beyond surging in primal
      unison,
      waxing and waning
      infinitely fickle,
whether warming or stunning,
sprightly or deadly, measured
      as the diastolic,
      systolic rhyming
of harmonious lust
         timing
      one's abrupt
passage through the narrows.

Storm

"There's storm on the horizon far,
The sun grows cold and dim,
I fear the snow will settle down
Before I make it in."

And sure enough before I'd made
The inner islands' lee,
The snow storm came a-roaring in
And blanketed the sea.

The wild wind lashed the mountain waves
And creamed their crests with foam;
And I set the compass bearing
For what I thought was home.

All I could do was hold her bow
Into the biting wind and snow.
I could not tell what my bearings were
Where I was headed I didn't know.

I steered for a thousand hours
Through the blinding, swirling white.
So close it was I could not tell
If it was day or night.

The angry waves came towering high,
Dwarfing my little boat; they crashed

Hard on the shivering cabin front.
The windshield glass was cracked, then smashed.

The seas that broke on the cabin top
Poured in through the gaping hole;
And half the sea was in my boots,
And my clothes were stiff with cold.

Toward each new crest we struggled up;
And each new wave in fury smote
The battered, plunging, straining bow,
Burying foam over my helpless boat.

All night the blinding blizzard raged;
And all night long I fought the storm,
Thinking each wave would be the last,
Wondering if I'd see the dawn.

So low the hope ebbed in my heart,
On that wild and desperate ride,
That when I used gas from the spare gas cans,
I hove the empties over the side.

Then straight ahead a shadow dim
Rose up from out the sea;
The cruel rocks were ringed with white
And reaching out for me.

The shoreline seemed familiar,
So, I followed it, creeping slow;
And glad I was when the harbor lights

Came faintly out of the snow.

It was four a.m. by my pocket watch
When I got in that night;
The harbor never looked so good,
Nor the harbor lights so bright.

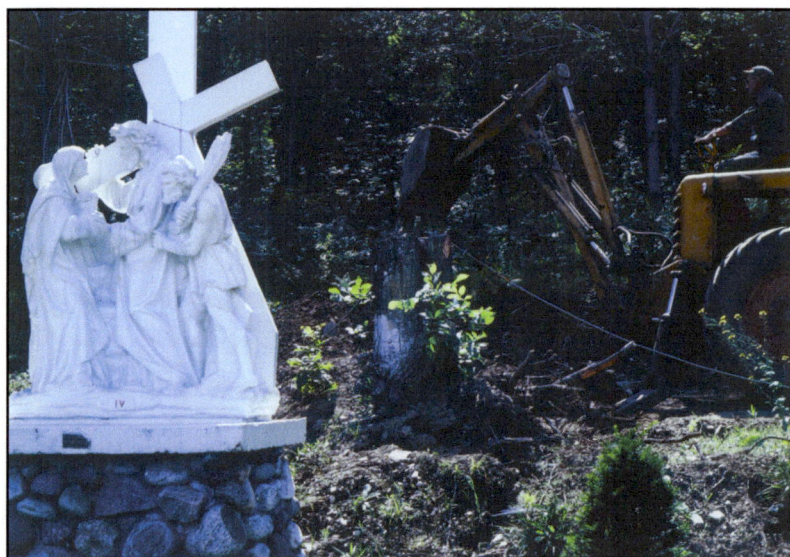

Earth Movers

The morning air was turning
blue with a film of diesel stench torn
by the crackling downfall of monumental
pines blazed for a king, belching
bulldozers backing and filling
with carnivorous gluttony as man—
tempered steel bit into cataclysmically
basted granite—ungodly, unheeded
shrieks foretasting doomsday's orgy:
the leftover bones nudged into a common
grave, a grisly jumble of skeletal
kindling awaiting the lime.

Scrabbling there in the debris, quick
as a pair of puma cubs cavorting
in Wild Kingdom's radiant Chromacolor,
their delight in the imagined havoc
a chirping commentary on the job at hand,
sharing a playful project as craftily
engineered as a corporate scheme reduced
to Tonka Toy scale, casually unearthing
mighty boulders hatched from stones
no bigger than larks' eggs:
pretending it was a spur
to I-95 perhaps.

Patiently rooted standing watch, mind adrift:

eyes idly following the spooked flight
of a shag flapping seaward from the far
bend of the marsh, my only intrusion, other
than this, was to warn them to detour
around the flower bed up ahead, a wistful
outcropping of pubescent tender
peony sprouts ringed by Jason's mother
with whitewashed paving blocks
pilfered from the dead
quarry on Crotch Island.

Fission

Hardy as mesquite, rank
as vetch, the errant weed
blooms with riotous vitality
mocking the morbid landscape.

Imagine the harvest to be
reaped could we harness, deadly
foe as ally, the radiant
energy of the exuberant
biomass flourishing at the expense
of nearby lung, breast
or bowel.

TLC

This morning's glance
to the whiskers, anticipating
the embalmer's blade, sharpened
her vision of iron into a surreal
insight; The stubble, a shade
grayer than those concave cheeks,
had thickened overnight. The rank
outcropping of that hideously robust
tumor crowding a temporal lobe
into terminal apathy?

Either that visit or during
another of those countless trips
to look in on him, perhaps
feeling under the sheet to finger
the catheter, hoping for his sake
to be greeted by name, she relapsed
into vain nostalgia recalling
the uncountable times his old spiced
cheek had grazed hers, a breast—
her navel, then on down
beyond the mockery
of that fruitless linea alba
to her eternally wistful thighs,
being addressed all the while
in the rasping gutterals of enticed lust.

Her insistent salutation as welcome, surely,
as the diffident hello of that fetching
wraith, mask tipped to tempt
a daredevil kiss, the ritual probe
of a tomboy tongue, or more often
simply the companioniable bug of soulmates
adrift in loneliness, fleshing out
the soft, clingy camouflage donned
in the latest of those periodic dreams
sampling a fondness for one another
they had been schooled to dread.

At the window, knees tensed
against the sill, haphazardly
watching a lone junco down
below frantically bobbing for
seeds in a clutter of leaves,
Lorna was reminded anew of life's
best kept secret in peace as well
as war. Perhaps to mute the clamor
of Paul's lopsided breathing, she heard
herself wail, not uttering a sound: "Oh,
Christ, I'm left once again with nothing
but a vested interest
in a loved one's death."

Chance Polarity

Savor all those darting scares,
piranha in the chlorinated pool,
that piece away on your aplomb
slong the route of a given day:
That panic bar that refuses to give
with the frantic when the demagog
high above in the mezzanine boasts
he sniffs smoke. The thumb-daubed
old-fashion tumbler lofted in time
with the Angelus, teeming with flawed
E. coli colonizing with logarithmic
zeal. The express lift speeding hell
bent to the 69th floor twitches in flight,
winking the light with executionaer's
glee, prompting your empty vitals
to sag with false gravida as you envision
a maloccluded cog, a loosend bolt,
or what once traded as the devil's
chicanery, or gods' wrath, threatening
to plummet you—attached case, dittoed
presentation, the night's labors—straight
as a dead weight on a shrieking return
trip to the filth-splattered pit below.
But should you ever hanker to lower
yourself down to a hearty feast
of terror, honor the appointment
in the morning with the balding

dentist whose curious wife you may
have known in passing.
Being pried ajar, outflanked by sleek
cutlery, mask askew, lips chafed
and drooling wry wider at his squat—
fingered cuem until knuckled agape
in ungainly accouchement, hearing
the sibilant dacron of his tunic
stalking the drape as he enters the glistening
auger fathoms deep into your tongue–
tied whimper to scavenge the gnawing rot.
Oddly rapt glances feud, a stunted gasp
in gutterals drowning in phlegm, wet
palms grate, nails skewer between cramped
breaths as his lunge shifts
for leverage, his sanguine grunts a pro
forma couvade, mocking your muffled,
diastolic yelps of spreadeagled dread.
Primly snarling past the worn facade,
the bezerk device is brought to bear
at last on your unsheathed pulp, bonding
the cybernetic synapses, *Yahwe!* forking
amperes of luciferous pain to the far
metes of your taut and pulsing grid.
Aaah, Mother of God, a primal ache freed!
Fused thus in platonic rapport, proxy
culprit and gloating victim, a harrowing
splice effete as asepsis can make it,
you're now positive to the scored
core of your field that he was the last
to know, metering the droning ohms and abroad

sheets, that he's scorned home and abroad
as that most ludicrous of current cuckolds.

Recylcing

The skull, a grimace burnished
to headstone gray, sundered from its train
of vertebra and shanks, was quickly
seen for what it was: a collectible
to be added to the trove a scavenger
his age treasures with a greed no longer
wholly innocent.

As we trudged on down the fire road,
Sven's spry curiosity about life and
its diversions was fleetingly
sidetracked by the sudden arc of a
tardy flicker from singed larch
to stubborn-leafed oak, the last
of the ominously pitched splinters
of sunlight prettily enflaming the dying
sumac embers.

Dawdling behind listening to my own flesh
and blood toying with reasons why with cues
from his straightforward mother—the fawn's stark
visage clutched in a casual bowler's grip—
I was grateful that fate had fashioned
it so that the maggots, death's agnostics,
had long since come and gone
to wherever they go to wait, tidy
communion done.

Mise-en-Scene

See, little man: This pine seedling
wading a puddle of melt appears
to have weathered the mad solstice,
ridiculing, from January's labored entrance
to furious exit, your father's fireside
boasts of prairie blizzards; a split
branch it's only visible wound, sad
as that grounded junco's wing, remember
last fall under the suet we hung?

Maybe broken, Muriel, by the winter-long
tread of an arctic cat, that mutagenic
new cult of predators we imagined,
cabin feverish under our dual-temp cover,
bootlessly prowling the sepulchral night
woods, stampeding yarded deer too spindly
to flee with the ear-feathered hares?

Over here, you two: April's glib tongue,
coarsened by leftover highway brine,
has lapped through the flank
of this wasting drift, baring
the blooded pelt of some post-Darwinian
varmint, which on flinching scrutiny
might turn out to be nothing but more
of our mounting scoria, a cast-off diaper?
Look at it this way, family: Come July,

that hibernating pair of Falstaff cans
will offer communal haven to a colony
of slugs—shady kin we bony ingrates
seek to keep at a distance?
The doggedly blithe Sunday
hunt is eventually rewarded
at Echo Lake's marshy end:

Sven's footdragging doubts were stilled
first by his mother's beckon,
but it remained my throwback role to mimic
a frontiersman with the longest reach,
playing armed provider harvesting
with whetted blade the immaculately
tumescent willows, a pathetic fallacy
condoned, dare I trust? by the script
torn from the calendar above our sink.

Lost at Sea Crossing the Bar

The black toe
of my boot idly sets
adrift the scarf of Irish
moss hung in the storm's wake
to drape blunt as crepe in the high
glass morning a worm pocked piling, as I
seek to fathom the sea's recent toll peering
down from the sighing wharf at the weather
beaten hull in which two fishing men—
broke down in that hell's moat off
Schoodic—died embracing
each other's
terror.

The stare aloft
by the three fingered
stranger grieving at my bent
elbow, wryly beckoning the downwind
scurry of the unsheepish clouds bound
home, confirms for us both in the tongue
thickened eulogy due the lost and the
leaving that the backside gale will
die with the sun and the morrow
will be another fit day
to sit out clutching
our watered
doubts.

Pretty Marsh Ambush

Stationed among the aloof spruce
and cedars, hounded by a savage
posse of Culicidae out for blood,
is a creepy brown VW on a long
detour off the Autobahn to chance
upon this dim path overrun by adder
tongued fern and fetching nightshade
worn down generations ago by a file
of Abenaki enroute to the clam digs below.

(The beetle driver, disguised in tight
crotched bells and Sesquicentennial beard,
fondly winks at a jowly squad of High
Life drinkers joylessly lobbing tinsel
into the alder suckers to twinkle
like bayonet tips for what will seem
forever in others' paranoia.)

His duty today, as it has been all this mad
season, is to seek to waylay the unwary
clutch of young spies say haunt this glen
for pot parties (aha!) with frantic hopes
of patching in on the primal vibrations
given off by the tumorous spruce, the wried
cedars, the crushed ferns and spilt blood
red berries, the dogged tread of the last war
painted brave to stalk this way

in that previous scene
of kindlier roles.

Panacea

As if to mock our tries, the old take
an unconscionable time to die,
making sure that no matter what we attempt
the choice is terrible, leaving us aside
the grave stricken with malaise that responds
to no remedy except the one before us.

Shell Game

The blackwinged gull on a bombing
run, conned by eons of cunning,
hung as a fleur-de-lys in a field
of blue stopped at f-500, flung
the mussel down to the sea weary ledge.

But, alack, what had promised to be
a tasty plunder was seen to be
on heeled approach nothing but
a fractured, lifeless blunder,
an artifact of sand and grit.

The supperless gull beat
off into the sanguine sundown
with pensive tacks toward Tinker's
Island, pondering, for all we know,
the deadly cracks in its logic.

Residuum

A gully
brought into fruition
by erosion

& Forbidden Fruits
seen corroding
teach us etiquette

When first we spoke
I stole
a pomegranate from your tree
It corrodes once
I eat it

at the edge of a gully
In your patience
I read how

warmth has potential here

Huge with our words we
speaking in circles recite
 for each other
4 sonnets

I'd go to the moon
for you

Did & took of the sphere
two pieces warm
in my hands
before they cooled

I was loving you a poem
with pomegranate lips—
—slick, now sediment, they too,
current at the soles
of my feet

I'm thinking of a boy
seeing The Moon; two pieces
of the giant
cooling his hands
Standing in a gully there
reciting himself
how, after picking a corpse
it still warms his throat

The last we spoke
You called me a thief

A piece of me sediments
at the bottom of a gully
after corroding

The boy is reciting to no one
how the last bite
of a ruby fruit
sweetens erosion

My body wants
to be the dry-land you edge
still warm in the place
we serenaded a sedimenting gully
          to fruition

There, a pomegranate
in a tree
looks down where a boy
tipped toes a reach
for its nape
with warm hands

When last I saw you
I offered a pomegranate
You said "tastes better
for you" and peeled
back the skin

I ate a pomegranate
It corrodes in my throat
Sedimenting our sonnets

My body—
corpse still warm before
cool

Here, in a gully once
huge with our words
Sonnets circle — how they
became sediment

& we commence
erosion

Heirloom

Undaunted brown eyes catch
at my hoarse yell, fixed
in that awful gap
between do and don't,
bestowing fingers age, as quickly
deaden, dropping the cutglass vase.

Toes cringe amid bedside debris:
Gleaming, bioodthirsty splinters,
cyanotic asters and fractured straw
flowers arranged this morning
by his mother as one more
milestone of my interim recovery.

Lonely Union

Too far gone now to turn his head
even to watch, he monitored Jo's
diligent grunts as she went on
alone that futile midnight, free
hand limp on his clammy thigh
while he stared at the writhing
ceiling awaiting her despairing whine
of triumph, no longer curious
as to unspeakable wishes
she might be making come true to efface
the lie to horrible past and terrifying
future long enough for them to enjoy
this stunted facsimile of their love.

Pursuing to Its Cul-de-sac the Cold Trail Blazed by the Grousing Portnoys

This yelp is provoked by the prosaic
libertines who abuse the frank for hire.
Those finicky new blue noses
newly licensed to job the apocalyptic
jest of its Joycean zest, the polichinellean
prank of its Shandean delights,
rubbing *our* noses in the literal,
cinder-strewn littoral of their despair
of ever forging Tartarean magma
again from T. Sterne's pince-nez tailings.

Abrading the lot of us
with graphite cant, they've heisted
the scrim from our privates, blown
the piquant whiff from Panope's briny pleats,
ravished the spiraling conundrum
of its Elizabethan stunts,
tarnished the chivalric tricks
of the Arthurian Rone, alas.

Where once the gentle reader,
making the drone of one hand applauding,
bloomed the supple groin to a privy fancy,
we're left, *Alcinoo poma dare*,
with the Chaucerian rejoinder, (another
pathetic fallacy, monumentally indigenous,

defaced): there's nothing more redundant
than a doxy's dugs hawked
as an encore.

So mourn today's Daedalus, stackworn,
circumscribed, thrice beggered, bereft of alchemy.
(Agapenome's coverts crisped to a desert,
coy Erato deflowered, stammers, blushes
at last, flushed from ambush by CBW.)

Stript of the mummery of Harlequin motley,
he's denied the host of assonant spoofs
that served the pioneering old shysters
so euphemistically, those sixty-nine
stations of ambiguity's cross, the sly
hocus-pocus of caroming innuendoes inciting
the avid audience to wanton synergism, sweaty palmed
footpads burgling the lid of the id.

Passe, too, are all those two-ply pawns
thumbed from Funk and tattered Wagnalls
to stalemate (heady ploy!) the jowly queen
and spleeny bishop guarding the fold
of Billingsgate.

Prospero limp, who remains to toll
perchance the clanging allusion,
eerie as yon clapper in hither fog?

Foreshortened by hindsight,
no writer now would be so callow

as to risk Uncle Walt's puckery chuckle
from abaft the ichor-filigreed leaves
by titling the tale of two tipling striplings
closeted against a Superior gale,
"The Three-Day Blow," as did the young Papa
salving his old nicks and chronic bruises.

Or, more urbanely, play hide and seek tongue
in cheek with a school of post-Hegelian giddies
who made believe Franny Glass actually froze
in the sphinctered throes
of the hymeneal epiphany, stalled, uncannily
beholden on a gratis crapper,
while in the darkening wings Brother Zooey
whistled the last refrain of J.D. Haydn's *Stabat Mater*
in memory of lame duck Seymour who met his timely
end cocking his piece after going down
to sea with a salty little pussy
having the time of *her* time on the crackling
stock of the hygienic New Yorker.

Or, truly plucky, should he seek
to flex the subtly webbed liberties
Yeats braved in his derring-do swansong,
'terrified vague fingers pushed the feathered glory
from her loosening thighs,' shudders!
he'd be hissed, *caput mortuum!*
from the workshop crestfallen!

Original metaphor marked down to deadpan
hairsplitting, sin remains synthetic,

finally fobbed of its Celtic graces
and orphaned guilt, dogged
as Kartaphilos, peeps in
through our brittle
aerosoled
panes.

Urges

Poets, true
lovers, heed the sea;
that constant beckoning to
flee staid landings
       until old bearings
       are lost,
looming anew in the deeps
beyond through which
pulses the lunar lure,
       waxing and waning
       infinitely fickle,
whether warming or stunning,
sprightly or deadly, measured
       as the diastolic,
       systolic rhyming
of harmonious lust tolling
       one's abrupt
passage through eternity.

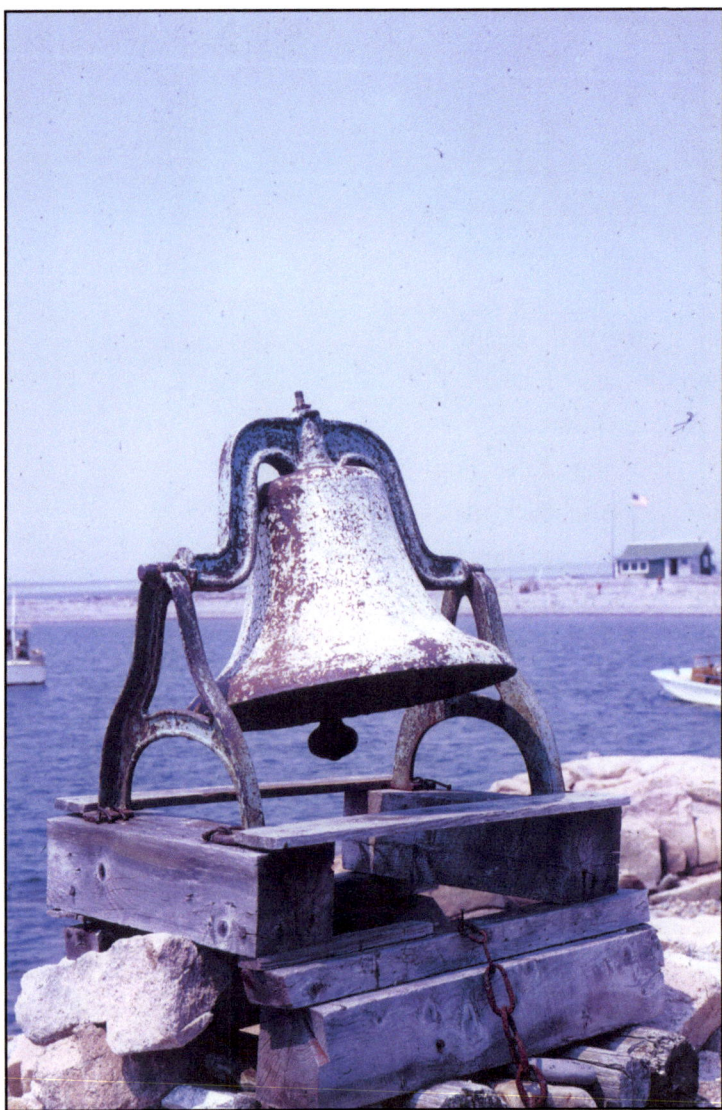

In Another Country

Once through Customs,
I greeted the waiting youth
with Gallic lubricity
flush on his chapped lips
in thanks for the unstruck
blows of twenty-odd years
since he first brandished a
fist so purely enraged my
awe hid behind its opposite.
Why the foolhardy kiss?
Having waived his love
with errors of omission
earning his ready scorn
to my tardy remorse, I
had come, too wise now
to beg, to bargain finally
for his prudent affection
with the reckless meter
of my chaotic heart.
All I dared hope, seeking
no armistice with tears
while his fingers felt my
cheek for a wary instant
echoing-with-possibilities,
is that his shame will
be tempered by time
before he is left

behind to look back on his
own, as all fathers must

if the Furies be evenhanded.

My Blue-Eyed Wife, Yes

             In all the race of Cain
             there is none
             with an ancestry as corrupt
             as mine.
I stencil your legacy with the forgiving
             barter of grievances
in this fierce showering of my indelibly
             bastard genes.
             Being a man I have but
             two chances,
             including love, to redeem
             my cursed lineage.
Our child and his will know their fathers
             stood armed
to risk patricide rather than to go on dying
             blanched replicas
             of unfaced evil.

The Salinity of Ocean Park

This is what leaving
San Francisco looks like
but, I'm back now, and
coming home flown me over
tidal pools
A congregation of colored water masses
       Tinged by salt; Microorganisms
—they prefer *Microalgae*
Color determined of tolerant
for salinity This spectrum
made arriving *Ocean Park*
Landing strip laid by Diebencorn
       —Bay air seasoned of Matisse
Salinity conjures language on the tongue
An easy sprout

Offspring

"And if they only knew. They lean on
me constantly. Like smiling bravely,
quote, unquote, when I split with nothing
but my Linus blanket."
"I know. Mine are just as heavy.
Mother starts to explain her side,
the Old Man turns us both off,
saying it's my life, it's not
worth a scene."

"Mom still calls me 'Baby'"
"Dad calls me 'Sono.' Maybe they've never
enjoyed the sound of our names?"
"How'd you happen, love,
have any idea?"
"I've given it some thought lately."
"I absolutely know I was a mistake, coming
so late. Mother confessed as much,
being so fantastic that time
she found my pill prescription."

"You didn't tell them how
we've opted not to choose
the time or place, I hope."
"Never. That would be *too* smug."
"And terrifying. Like free will."
"... Or natural childbirth, right?"

"I don't want to disturb you,
but are we done with the pillow?
...Ah, thanks. But you don't think
you were an accident?"
"You've met my father. Anal as a computer,
insurance poor. Jesus, he's dead
set against credit cards even."

"Which is worse? Being after-the-fact
gaffes they had to learn to love?
Unwelcomed side effects of horny..."
"... Or planned investments? Hardheaded,
strategically timed ripoffs from the
Zero Population Crusade? Christ, talk
about economic determinism."
"Makes us sound like livestock, that way.
Or sired by champion studs."

"What the hell, girl, maybe our maculate
conceptions didn't matter. We're carrying
on—evolution's new elite. Free agents,
beholden to nobody. I mean..."
...Dropouts from the word go.
"Of course. And with Oedipus supposedly
dead and buried with the bloody
hatchet, relatively sound in mind and body."

"According to my doctors... But the fucking
circumstances *do* have a bearing, sweet.
Otherwise, where's our one earthly chance
to get out of our skins

and try for a miracle?"
"You got me. Down the drain probably.
Are you about ready for a Kleenex?"

"Not right yet. Unless you're beat.
This is such a precious feeling, Aaron.
So close, yet so spacious. Like a lull
between ticking catastrophes. I'd love
to make it last forever and ever."
"Who knows, Kathy? Maybe we have."

Summer Gypsies

Feetfirst, cheek buried in Ron's moldy
sheepskin, Greg was sleeping off last night's fog
shrouded frolic when Kay, changing shirts
alongside, recognized their destination miles ahead.
She pointed, swiveling pliantly from her lotus
squat, to the crown of Katahdin jaggedly
framed by the picket of spruce, a few relic
pines, as they panned by over the potholed blacktop.

John Paul, hunched against the back
of the front seat wading through the urine
yellowed (lobster juice, don't you imagine?)
blindman's edition of the *Times* scavenged
from an Acadia garbage can, tugged at the Y
of his napless cords to reshuffle *Lebensraum*
for his chronic busriders' erection, grunted,
went back to the extinct news, still odd man out.

Next to the window up front, Alan felt down
into his gadget bag for the long lens to his
Hasselblad, ignoring Judi's yawning reminder
they had been out of film since their last batch,
hustled panhandling bemused French Canadians
at Old Orchard Beach, had been wiped out shooting
candids of that credibly drunk paraplegic
of World War Two Vintage at Boothbay.

Cursing, writhing in his wheelchair like an amputee
octupus, bulbous torso bared, the invalid had finally
managed to overpower his mortified wife; his traveling
companion anyway, curlers vibrating like pastel
leeches as she staggered back empty handed.

Noncommittal, schizoid as marks ogling a carnival
geek, they watched him heave, venting a godawful
wail of triumph, his colostomy pouch over
the barrier and into the harbor where it hit
with the queasy clap of a culled flounder.

Rare victory won, the ripped off graybeard wheeled
with the ferocious, detoured vim of his ilk
across the spongy parking area to the shimmering
Airstream with black on white Nebraska plates.

The Micro braked to a stop, Ron grabbed
the emptied Chablis bottle in Judi's lap
and plying it as a make believe 'scope
scanned the distant mountain peak until
he found what he sought, then thrust it
back at her, swearing: "You can see the dried
and frozen carcass of the leopard off
to the left, just below the summit."

An unfrocked English major too, Greg
stirred and groaned, but made no effort
to rise and see the Kilimanjaro mirage.
Instead, he reached out to finger a tiny gray worm
of blanket ravel from the coils of

Kay's navel. Perhaps because proffered
immediately above, her nipples, gauchely chipper
in the morning after chill that only deepened
his downer, were seen in hallucinated flash
back as miniature tent pegs, gnarled, blunted,
mushroom headed by savage blows of a hatchet
enraged by the inhospitality of the hard
scrabble till they had encountered more often
than not on this safari that had begun
as a unanimously carefree whim and might
conceivably end the same way, with luck.

Unless, confounditall, Judi kept demanding
as a matter of principle invoked belatedly
as was her communal privilege the fifth week out,
that Alan share her with the others
again, now that she had consented to play
it straight, promising them all to put in
for a Dee & Cee at the Beaver St. Clinic
the moment they got back to New Rochelle,
around Labor Day as now vaguely programmed.

Sorry, Pops

Our parting, my Dad and I, was an old scene
to the undeniable black attendant
more concerned with the smudge of ash
on the white sleeve of his Dacron tunic
than with an old man's passing history,
an optimism doomed to failure,
of seeking to acquire with eager hand and
wistful cheek the respect he lacked the guile
and arrogance to extract by force.

Or so it seemed for years spent
indentured in the service of others,
taking orders back when grocery story lists were thrust
across wooden counters, erasing teachers'
graffiti from after school blackboards before going
down to work the plunger to free a stranger's stool
back in the days before janitors were
known as custodians, until the war boom came along
to promote a handyman, with a feel for wood,
to the rank of journeyman carpenter, a plastic
union card his proud badge of admission
to the hiring hall whose kinship
to the slave market he never considered
until the housing boom slacked off and the five bucks
an hour, the job foremen dared pick and chose
again, discarding the slow and slowing down,
leaving the Federation porkchopper with nothing

left to say but "Sorry, Pops, Nothing for you
again today."

Graveled Pits

The mounds in stark midday loom
as stricken whales beached
beside their tumbled graves
bloated dun remains leaching
bile into rainbowed pools
of stale scum attended again
by patient snakes lurking
among the sorry lupine,
the three wan willows.

While the lid of one bewildered
eye remains shut to the raining dust
the brazen sun times its glide
to spot its prey with its infernal
glance interred deep in the voluptuous
spoils of ice-wrought till
daring the bent handle of a rusting
spoon to sparkle with abandoned glee,
fey as the wink of a spent star.

Generation of Peace

Herded through Customs,
I greet my stoic host
with abrupt abandon flush
on his faintly glistening
tautly neutral lips
in thanks for the unstruck
blows of twenty five years
since he flailed out at
an emptied breast with a
smeary fist so purely enraged
our awe hid behind its opposite.

Why the stone sober kiss—lancing
withdrawal pangs of a nitro
hungry heart unheeded—branding
me an accomplice in public
view here at the Toronto jetport?

Having deserted his love
pursuing choices of my own,
I had come, too empty-handed
to bribe, to bargain finally
for his prudent allegiance,
all tokens squandered
but an eyewitness account
of his mother's committal.

All I dare hope, seeking
no armistice with tears
while his fingers trace
their course for a haunted
instant monstrous with old
betrayals, is that this son
I'd hounded into exile might
embrace me in the blanket
clemency his age may wish
to bestow once we're safely
dead or dying.

Five O'clock High

Across the cove, spruce stand stars
as a cortege of nudes congealed
in Warhol stop action: free
hand cut outs of black, filigreed
by hackmatack etchings, steely
wreaths for the worm riddled
dory beached to die below,
backlighted by the bloody hues
of a withdrawing sun: incongruous
Polynesian sheen on midwinter nimbus
paleing to saffron, an arc of acetylene
green braises Raphael rosy flanks,
hectic blush stains, drains, while quaint
vestal fleshtints flame out in a spasm
of holocaust crimson as night emerges
piecemeal on ash drab blotches
of cumulus, tatters of a past gale.
Erased last are the prettied up
graffiti: mawkish Playboy pinks burlesquing
split lips, chilled areolae, open bed
sores, slashed by a programmed pair
of phantom jets whose pilots on a needle
nosed heading to westward are still
monitoring the livid heavens above
and beyond the darkened cove, junked
hulk shrouded by the evening tide.

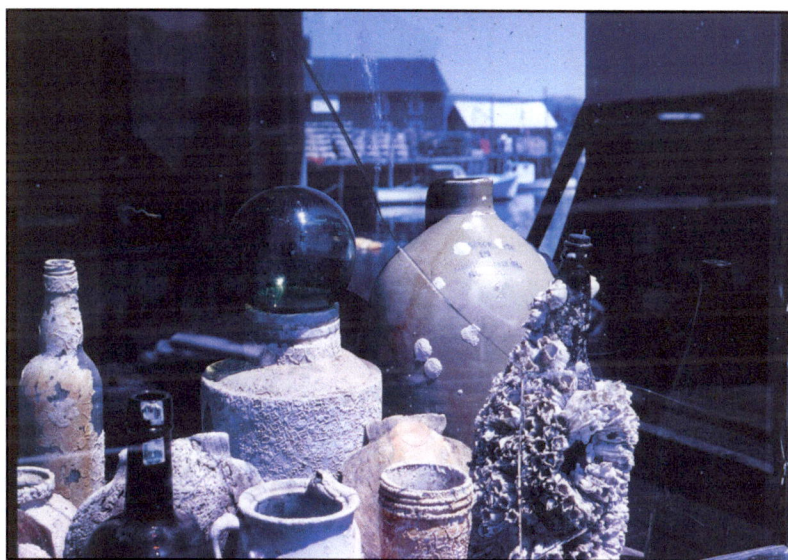

Trade Secrets

With true regard for the others who stocked the eddies, here's a
    creel filled with keepers, lifting the best lines, from the
    spring freshet of the big two-hearted river called the
    Kennebec, Col. VI:

An impress in the common geography
of our hearts of an old forgotten love
leaving a print as rhetoric,
an arched addendum:

In a gamble for the memory when
something like a response may thrive,
you were primed for bed in that garden
of great renown down by the marsh,
held there by a trick of light between
the squash and succotash.

A maimed juggler clapping with one
hand touched by an old admonitory
demon, prancing wishes causing a cerebral
rash, back bent like a bow, teeth bared
above the quill until end-rhymes leak
at your lips like spiced sanguinity,
this new lover named loneliness,
in fingering reach of flesh pinched
into folds, but remembering patches
of snow, contours silvered with ice,

feigns a righteous non-violent plunge
into unctuous hell fired to chase
the descended cold.

Chilled by 'die Beschwerde langen
Lernens,' I will not see
Venus curling to whirl me, still
with death, into the space held
open by the crescent moon. The right
of first refusal belongs to me. Won
by will? Or fantasy?

Letter to Terry Plunkett

All through college I moonlighted as a flunky in an Iowa City funeral home. I'm allergic to the stench of carnations to this day. That's where I first saw that the cosmetic reconstruction of a shotgun victim's visage, say, could be seen as a variation of artistry, if a trifle macabre.

But the embalmer at the establishment was hardly a lonely homozygous Donald Mason. To his wife's bereavement, he was the randiest philanderer I'd encountered til then. It was as though he was driven by his clammy and stark naked stock-in-trade to keep sampling the warmer wares at the opposite end of life's spectrum. A not uncommon, and forgivable, occupational hazard among morticians...

My fleeting association with that profession, as it likes to be known, made indelible on later reading Camus' declaration during the French Resistance that he could forgive God any death but that of a child.

Speaking of deities: While I never could spell for sour owlshit, the effort to use words precisely is the nearest to a religion I have left. We all fall from grace a little now and then, hardly a mortal sin.

Cheers, and carry on...

Last Words

Thanks world
for everything
FRD

Photo courtesy Sven Davisson

www.ingramcontent.com/pod-product-compliance
Lightning Source LLC
Chambersburg PA
CBHW041531090426
42738CB00036B/113